6502

Waffen-SS

(2) From Glory to Defeat 1943-1945

Text by Robert Michulec
Color plates by Ronald Volstad

CONCORD
PUBLICATIONS COMPANY

Editor: James Hill

by CONCORD PUBLICATIONS CO.
603-609 Castle Peak Road
Kong Nam Industrial Building
10/F, B1, Tsuen Wan
New Territories, Hong Kong

We welcome authors who can help
expand our range of books. If you
would like to submit material,
please feel free to contact us.

We are always on the look-out for new,
unpublished photos for this series.
If you have photos or slides or
information you feel may be useful to
future volumes, please send them to us
for possible future publication.
Full photo credits will be given upon
publication.

ISBN 962-361-632-5
printed in Hong Kong

Introduction

Following the defeat of the German forces at Stalingrad in January 1943 and the increase in the Soviet counter-offensive in January and February, the German Army needed a victory to regain its momentum. Such a victory came in March when the SS Panzer Corps recaptured Kharkov.

Because of the reputation acquired by the Waffen-SS divisions and their armored units as a result of the Kharkov success, Hitler was determined to use them as much as possible throughout the remainder of the fighting in Russia. By the time the German summer offensive got underway, the Waffen-SS had expanded and the SS divisions had been redesignated as Panzer (armored) divisions. The infantry came to be known as Panzergrenadiers (mechanized infantry).

Because of its high mobility and proven record as a hard, dedicated combat unit, the Waffen-SS was employed as a kind of fire brigade to plug gaps in the lines of the vast Eastern Front. The leaders of the regular German Army had a great appreciation for the reliability of the SS troops. After the invasion at Normandy, six SS Panzer divisions were sent to attempt to push the Allies back into the Atlantic. The SS participation in the Normandy Campaign took a toll on the Waffen-SS. The young soldiers in the 12.SS-Panzer-Division 'Hitlerjugend', for example, suffered 60% casualties during the four weeks of fighting there.

The Waffen-SS underwent an interesting change later in the war. As the numbers of racially pure SS members dwindled, and as it became increasingly necessary to fill the ranks, more and more non-Germans were admitted into the ranks of the Waffen-SS. Those recruited included volunteers from Scandinavia, Belgians, Norwegians, Yugoslav Muslims, Hungarians, and even some conscripts from France and Russia.

Following the end of the war and the Nuremberg Trial, the reputation of the Waffen-SS as a formidable fighting force was tarnished by the participation of SS units in a number of atrocities, such as the massacres at Malmédy and Oradour-sur-Glane. Nevertheless, during the fifty years since that time, military historians and hobbyists have been fascinated by the combat performance of the Waffen-SS . . . and there is no indication that this interest will diminish in the next half century.

ACKNOWLEDGEMENTS

All photographs published in this book are from: Military Institute of History; Central Military Archives; Military Photo Agency; Central Photo Archives; and the author's collection. I would like to thank Tomasz Kopanski, Seawek Gonera and the crews of the mentioned institutions for their help, support and patience.

With the cityscape of the captured Russian city of Kharkov rising behind them, the bodies of two dead Soviet soldiers lay frozen in the foreground as a mute testimony to the success of the SS troops, particularly the 'Leibstandarte Adolf Hitler' Division (LAH), who fought there in the spring of 1943. The part of the city where this photo was taken was called the 'Platz der Leibstandarte' in their honor.

SS men take cover in foxholes in a demolished Russian house in the Kharkov region. The holes were probably carved out of the cement during the hard-fought struggle to capture the city. Both the soldiers wear reversible camouflage jackets.

Three SS Panzergrenadiers (mechanized infantrymen) remove a red communist flag from its holder on a Soviet Party building following the capture of the city of Kharkov. Note that the soldier in the middle carries a Russian PPSh sub-machine gun.

The year 1943 brought an escalation of partisan operations throughout Europe, especially in occupied Poland where even the Jews had an uprising in the Warsaw ghetto. Among the Nazi troops who were tasked with suppressing the partisan activity and carrying out executions, the police units were the most brutal. This photo shows a mixture of police and SS troops taunting six men who were suspected of partisan activity. Their main armament is the MP28 sub-machine gun.

SS men dig in after taking up a position as part of an encircling cordon at the outskirts of a forest. Dressed in a camouflaged smock, the radio operator in the foreground sets up his equipment: a transmitter (with the antenna) and a receiver, a Totn. Fu. D (Tornister Funk D). Because of their size they had to be carried on the backs of two men.

Prior to the summer offensive of 1943, the Germans launched a number of anti-partisan operations of various scales, and many SS units were active participants. Here we see troops from an SS unit advancing through a forest clearing during a lull in the fighting.

The success of anti-partisan operations in the late spring/early summer of 1943 was limited, with the Soviet partisan movement suffering only minor defeats. The majority of the victims of the SS troops were civilians supporting partisans. Many of them were sent to concentration camps, but many others suffered summary execution when apprehended. Seen here is one of the SS men who took part in successful anti-partisan activity. He is examining an explosive pencil that was confiscated at a partisan base.

Far greater losses than those suffered during anti-partisan activity were inflicted on the Soviet military forces in July 1943 during Operation 'Zitadelle' (Citadel) — the Battle of Kursk. By the 16th of July, SS divisions had caused the death of thousands of Soviets. Thousands more were wounded and about 6,000 became POWs. On top of that, more than 500 Red Army soldiers deserted into SS hands.

Dressed in summer camouflage, an SS man with a range finder braves the heat of the July sun to give bearings on enemy targets to his gun crew. Billowing skyward in the background is smoke from an earlier direct hit.

After receiving information about distant targets, the crew of an 8.8cm Flak 18 antiaircraft gun belonging to the 'Totenkopf' Division prepares to fire deadly rounds of ammunition capable of demolishing any enemy target. The '88' was the most destructive tank-killing weapon used by the German troops, and all SS divisions had no less than a battery of these guns in their *Flak Abteilungen* (antiaircraft artillery detachments).

An '88' photographed at its battle position during the height of a gun duel with the enemy. So lethal was this weapon that no armored vehicle could hope to survive if found within the range of fire of the Flak 18 gun during the summer of 1943.

Seen here is the result of the deadly accurate fire from the 8.8cm Flak 18 gun. This Russian T-34 Model 1942 tank was shot to pieces somewhere in the southern part of the Soviet Union. Note the debris that was scattered all around the tank by the blast of the explosion.

A photograph of several more victims of German heavy artillery, which have blown the turrets right off the chassis of these Russian tanks. Shown here are the remains of three T-34 tanks with Model 1941 hulls, additional fuel tanks typical of the Model 1942, and hexagonal turrets that were introduced in late 1942.

It was during Operation 'Zitadelle' that the SS men first used self-propelled artillery in the regimental and divisional batteries. Seen in the background of this photo is one of three types of such vehicles from an SS unit — the Sd.Kfz. 138 'Bison' SPG. This vehicle was armed with the 15cm sIG 33 gun built on the Pz.Kpfw. 38(t) chassis and it was used in regimental artillery units of the Panzergrenadiers.

Waffen-SS reconnaissance troops advance on motorcycles. Such sub-units as these saw limited service during the fighting of 1943-1944 due to Soviet aggressiveness and the grand scale of fighting on the battlefield, where there was no place left for recce duties.

This close-up photograph, which puts us almost nose-to-muzzle with an SS 'Bison', shows many more details of the self-propelled gun. Though there is a name faintly visible on the armored plate of the superstructure's right side beneath the camouflage, it is not clear enough to read.

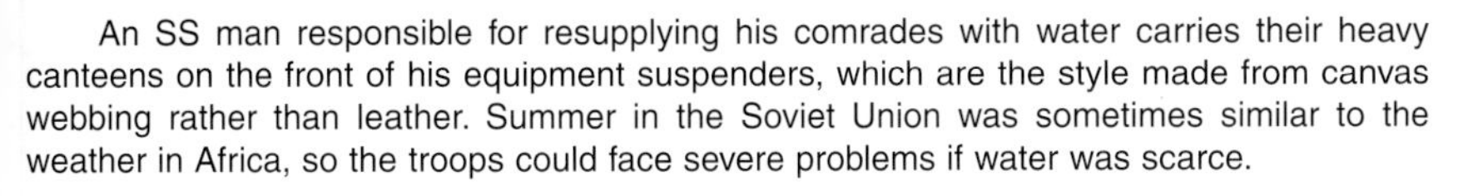

The BMW R75 heavy motorcycle with sidecar was probably the most versatile model of motorcycle used during the hard fighting of the summer of 1943. It was a fast and reliable supply vehicle. Here a three-wheeled 'supply column' delivers a load of bread to some grateful SS troops.

An SS man responsible for resupplying his comrades with water carries their heavy canteens on the front of his equipment suspenders, which are the style made from canvas webbing rather than leather. Summer in the Soviet Union was sometimes similar to the weather in Africa, so the troops could face severe problems if water was scarce.

Equipped with white-colored mine probes, a squad of engineers moves into action atop a StuG III Ausf. F from the 'Das Reich' Division. Note the interesting camouflage pattern on the assault gun. The markings (two vertical white bars over one horizontal white bar) on the vehicle's rear plate is the insignia for 'Das Reich' that was adopted prior to Operation 'Zitadelle'.

After having been delivered to the fray in a fast-moving Schwimmwagen amphibious vehicle, SS men of an MG42 machine-gun team leap into action in a sector of the front line that is being threatened by the enemy. There are recorded instances in battle when a small, quickly moving unit was able to check the advance of a larger enemy force thanks to the element of surprise and effective firepower.

More SS troops go into action aboard an armored vehicle, this time a Pz.Kpfw. III. Note the variety of weapons at their disposal —an MP40 'Schmeisser' sub-machine gun, an MG42 machine gun, and a Mauser Karabiner 98K rifle, as well as the manner in which the soldier in the rear carries his stick grenades.

Battle-weary troops are seen here taking a much-appreciated rest during a lull in the fighting. Their faces are a study in stoicism and determination, characteristics that came to define the men of the Waffen-SS as the campaign in Russia dragged on.

'Totenkopf' soldiers belonging to the divisional *Aufklärungsabteilung* (reconnaissance unit) wait anxiously to receive orders to advance. Note the helmet covers worn by the men on the upper left and lower right. This photo shows quite well how these camouflage covers were designed.

A lone SS man with an MG42 machine gun maintains cover on a battlefield abandoned by the Soviet armored troops. Thanks to the poor tactics used by the Soviets, the Germans were able to repulse the enemy's mass attacks while suffering only minor casualties.

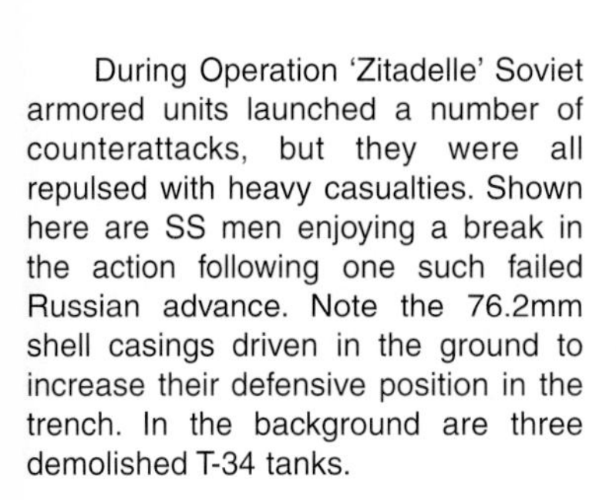

During Operation 'Zitadelle' Soviet armored units launched a number of counterattacks, but they were all repulsed with heavy casualties. Shown here are SS men enjoying a break in the action following one such failed Russian advance. Note the 76.2mm shell casings driven in the ground to increase their defensive position in the trench. In the background are three demolished T-34 tanks.

This SS radio team was photographed while operating behind the protection of an embankment. The ability to successfully communicate by radio or phone gave the Germans a distinct advantage over the Russians, who were poorly equipped when it came to such equipment.

Waffen-SS men prepare to do battle in a trench near Kharkov. This photo provides a good study of the variety of camouflage worn by the SS troops. The soldier in the middle wears a smock that combines both the 'palm tree' and 'plane tree' patterns, with the 'plane tree' pattern predominating.

One of the rules followed by soldiers throughout history is to never stay awake when one can sleep, and this machine-gun team traveling in a Schwimmwagen shows that anytime and anyplace is good for a nap. Note the tactical markings on the vehicle's hull next to what appears to be a hole made from a 20mm shell. Also interesting is the mount for securing the MG42 when not in use.

The rear view of an Sd.Kfz. 10 half-track equipped with a 2cm Flak gun that carries 16 victory markings on its barrel, all of which were won during 'Zitadelle'. However, this particular crew has to share the honors with the other crews in the battery. Note the 'Das Reich' marking of this period clearly visible on the hull.

Pz.Kpfw. IV Ausf. H tanks from II/Pz.Rgt. 'Leibstandarte Adolf Hitler' charge enemy positions in a formation that is typical of this period. Note the interesting pattern of the green camouflage on the nearest tank (number '546') and the other tanks in the distance.

SS-Hauptsturmführer (Captain) Vinzenz Kaiser (right), commander of 3rd Battalion in the 'Der Führer' Panzergrenadier Regiment of the 'Das Reich' Division, was photographed in front of a 'Churchill' heavy tank captured by SS troops during combat against the 5th Guards Tank Army in the Prokhorovka area between 12-15 July 1943. Kaiser was decorated with the *Ritterkreuz* (Knight's Cross) on 8 April 1943 after the successful fighting for Kharkov in February and March.

Soldiers of the 'Totenkopf' Division and a member of a Tiger tank crew consult a map as they advance in the direction of Prokhorovka. The Waffen-SS men are dressed in 'oak leaf' camouflage. Interestingly, the soldier with the Schmeisser slung behind his back seems to be wearing a set of camouflage overalls issued to crews of armored vehicles.

Waffen-SS officers from the 'Totenkopf' Division use binoculars to assess the effectiveness of fire from the Tiger tank seen in the above photo. By the middle of July 1943, the German Tiger and Panther tanks had taken a sizable toll against the Russian armored forces, but not enough to prevent a Soviet counterattack.

An SS sapper prepares a 'Teller Mine' antitank explosive for the enemy. Note the difference in color and style of his camouflage uniform. Of special interest is the helmet cover, which was pieced together from two different camouflage materials! His camouflage smock is the older style, while the trousers are from the drill camouflage uniform introduced in 1943.

As unlikely as it may seem, the 'Teller Mine' could serve as an adequate pillow when the need arose. Apparently grown accustomed to the proximity of explosives, this SS man also carries a stick grenade in his ammunition belt.

Making themselves as comfortable as possible, a group of Waffen-SS officers study an impressive array of maps. Considering the size of the Soviet Union, it is no surprise that so many of them were necessary. No doubt the bottle of dark liquid standing alongside the maps was used merely as a supplemental educational aid.

Here a group of officers discuss the upcoming action. Note the variety of headgear that includes the *Bergmütze* short-billed field cap (left-center), the *Feldmütze* sidecap (far right), and the M35/40 slate gray helmet featuring the SS-rune decal.

An SS gun crew mans a 7.5cm leIG 18 light gun after setting it up in position alongside a road in a Soviet village. This weapon was used on a regimental level for infantry support. Note the size of the ammunition it fires, an example of which is about to be loaded by the gunner in the center of the photo.

This photo provides us with a good study of the common soldier of the Waffen-SS and his typical appearance while in the field. Partially camouflaged in field of sunflowers to the left of the SS men is a 7.5cm PAK 40 antitank gun, which is aimed (oddly enough) in the direction of the flowers.

'Totenkopf' (Death's Head) Division soldiers help to push a truck out of the mud so it can deliver its load of supplies to the soldiers at the front. At the left is a soldier from a motorcycle unit who, unlike his fellow SS men pushing the truck, wears his bayonet at his right hip.

A break in combat affords this tank crew the opportunity to load ammunition into their Tiger tank. The tank has not been painted with any additional camouflage, but of special interest is the tactical number '1' that appears to have been applied with chalk. Note the difference is size between the rounds on the ground and the smoke candle dischargers at the bottom right of the photo.

Members of a *Sturmgeschütz* (StuG) self-propelled assault gun crew engage in a lively discussion about their mission while the crew's mascot looks on with curiosity. They both wear the dark gray-green uniform worn by assault gun crews, which was patterned after the black SS Panzer troop uniform.

A couple of war-weary SS men take some time to show a bit of attention to a couple of other mascots — a pair of rabbits. There is little doubt that they served in that role for only a short time since, like any other edible animals, rabbits would provide a nice break from the monotony of army food.

Photographed in the heat of combat, a crew member of a well-camouflaged SS PAK 40 gun loads an antitank round into the artillery piece. The PAK 40 provided the German Army a superiority over enemy troops that turned the tide of battle in their favor.

This photograph of the same PAK 40 was taken just after the gun had fired several well-aimed rounds at distant enemy tanks. There are no less than six columns of smoke rising in the background, which indicates that the crew must have destroyed some of their targets.

Seen here is a victim of the SS antitank-gun crews, a demolished T-34 Model 1942 tank with an old style of turret that featured side visors. By this time this model tank was no longer very dangerous to the German troops. The one seen here is one of dozens that were knocked out without any major difficulty.

German SS troops march in a long column as they advance across the Russian steppes. The soldier at the far left carries an MG42 machine gun in an unusual case. As in all wars, it is the soldier on the ground that usually determines the outcome of a battle.

Pictured here are the great trio of the 'Das Reich' Division. They are (left to right): SS-Standartenführer (Lieutenant-Colonel) Heinz Harmel, SS-Sturmbannführer (Major) Helmut Schreiber and SS-Hauptsturmführer (Captain) Gunter Wisliceny. They were photographed in Stepanovka on the 'Miusfront' in the beginning of August 1943. Schreiber was decorated with the Knight's Cross on 31 July 1943 for capturing a hill occupied by enemy troops that threatened the division's 'Deutschland' Regiment's flank. Wisliceny won his Knight's Cross on the same day for skillfully leading elements of his 3rd Battalion of the 'Deutschland' Regiment against enemy positions. He was wounded during the charge.

This is another shot of SS-Standartenführer Heinz Harmel, this time in the midst of battle while commanding from an Sd.Kfz 251 in August 1943. Harmel won his Knight's Cross on 31 March 1943 for successfully commanding the 'Deutschland' Regiment during the fight for Kharkov in February and the beginning of March of that year.

An SS Schwimmwagen slowly advances through the mire in a muddy stretch of land in Russia. If the terrain were any wetter, the driver would be compelled to lower the propeller at the rear of the vehicle to boost his speed. Note the markings that are visible just to the left of the propeller.

Congratulations are extended to SS-Unterscharführer (Sergeant) Hans Thaler from Pz.Rgt.2 of the 'Das Reich' Division who won the Knight's Cross on 16 August 1943 for destroying ten T-34s during nearly one hour of combat between three German and fifteen Soviet tanks. During the engagement his tank was damaged, but Thaler decided to repair it under enemy fire.

A group of 'Totenkopf' soldiers gaze skyward to watch German aircraft as they support their ground assault. In the background is a Pz.Kpfw. III. Note the tactical number on the turret and the camouflage scheme that it wears. It still exhibits the markings for Operation 'Zitadelle' even though that operation had ended by the time this photo was taken.

SS troops return from a reconnaissance mission across the Ukrainian steppes in the autumn of 1943. They are dressed in a mixture of camouflage smocks and overcoats. The smocks were usually worn by all combat sub-units, while the troops in the rear wore standard uniforms in field gray only.

Two different types of animals — a horse and a 'Tiger' — are seen in this photo that was taken in October 1943. The mounted soldier is a member of the 8th SS Kavallerie Division 'Florian Geyer' and the tank crewman is part of a mixed crew of Waffen-SS and Wermacht troops. 'Florian Geyer' was one of three SS cavalry divisions, but it was the most experienced and strongest, and it had the oldest traditions.

One of the most celebrated SS leaders was SS-Sturmbannführer (Major) Otto Skorzeny, whose Slavic roots allowed for his name to be pronounced as 'Skozhenni'. This photo of him was taken during a gathering at the *Berliner Sportpalaz* in October 1943. He won his Knight's Cross on 12 September 1943 for liberating the Italian dictator Benito Mussolini from captivity at the *Gipfelhotel* mountain lodge, even though the action was one of the worst prepared commando operations of WWII.

In October 1943, somewhere in the Karelian forests, a Wermacht soldier assists an SS stormtrooper with his Schmeisser MP40. The 6th SS Gebirgs Division 'Nord' mountain troops was originated in 1941 based on Kamfgruppe 'Nord' that was composed of two 'Totenkopf' regiments. It is no surprise that the poorly trained unit suffered heavy losses during the 1941 campaign. The SS man seen here wears a camouflage smock in the 'palm tree' pattern. Above his blackened face is seen the 1943 field cap. The soldier whose leg is visible in the background wears boots that are typical of mountain troops.

Here's dinner! Two Waffen-SS soldiers scramble over rubble in a ruined village somewhere in Russia. On there backs they carry containers of food for the troops of a front-line unit.

SS men silently negotiate a hillside as they cautiously approach the crest, unsure of what may be waiting for them on the other side. They are dressed in new reversible, padded winter suits that feature autumn camouflage on one side and white material on the other. Note the absence of field equipment.

One of the dozens of SS war correspondents who captured the thousands of photographic images for Third Reich and SS archives and publications. Soldiers of the *SS-Kriegsberichter*, or SS war correspondent unit (note the cuff title), usually performed their jobs on the front lines and were often involved in combat. The SS man shown here is one of those who tasted the real war and fought bravely, as his Iron Cross decoration attests.

Sitting in the 'hatch' of a specially prepared staff car, an SS non-commissioned officer waits to go into action. The vehicle has been painted in the standard two-color camouflage of an irregular green pattern over a sand undercoat. Just visible through the windshield is the driver of the car.

Hard at work. A fully loaded truck is used as a taxi by a solider of the combat photography unit, who carries a camera in his right hand, and another soldier for whom there was no room on the running board of the vehicle.

Two officers of a *Nebelwerfer* rocket launcher unit of the 'Totenkopf' Division synchronize their watches prior to going into action. Note the officer on the left, whose uniform is adorned with a German Cross in Gold on the right breast pocket, a Close Combat Clasp over his left breast pocket, and a *Demjanskshild*, the Demyansk campaign arm shield, on his left arm. All of these awards show him to be a brave and experienced soldier.

Soldiers carry a 15cm shell toward a Nebelwerfer 41 rocket launcher. This weapon was used for the first time in June 1941, almost a month before the Russians introduced their *Katjuscha* but it was not put into service with the SS troops until sometime later. Note the interesting camouflage painted on the weapon.

SS-Scharführer, 1st SS Panzer Division 'LAH', Eastern Front 1943

The fur-lined anorak worn by this NCO was a direct response to the lack of adequate clothing available the previous winter. It was normally issued with matching trousers that were commonly bloused into the boots. This clothing was unique to Waffen-SS troops and continued to be issued until war's end.

The anorak was initially a pull-over design made from rayon or canvas with a complete fur lining. Later versions were provided with a full length buttoned opening. Colors varied from slate gray to field gray to shades of olive green. Little effort was made in matching the fur pelts.

There were a number of detail variations related to pockets and hood size. Early hoods were large enough to be worn over helmets. When the front was left open for ventilation, the standard field gray uniform was visible underneath.

For snow camouflage, a simple white rayon smock was worn over the anorak. It is interesting to note that the Waffen-SS did not provide white helmet covers for winter. His gray wool gloves are standard issue.

The MP40 and magazine pouches are usual for an NCO along with the 6x30 binoculars. He is also carrying the magnetic Haft-Hohlladung 3kg Antitank Assault Charge.

SS-Pionier, 2nd SS Panzer Division 'Das Reich', Eastern Front 1943

By 1943 another variation of the camouflage smock was being issued. The Model 1942 (type 1) pattern differed from previous items by the inclusion of integral front pockets with buttoned flaps (almost hidden by the equipment) and the addition of foliage loops on the back and around the shoulders. The waist band was now placed higher. The oak leaf pattern was only one of the many used.

Hanging on his chest is a camouflage face veil. While not widely issued limited number of these were provided. When not used for face camouflage, these masks were flipped back over the helmet or worn as illustrated.

Also of limited issue was the Engineer Assault Pack. Only 20 percent of an engineer battalion would have received this gear (which was not unique to Waffen-SS troops).

All three items were made of olive green canvas. The belt pouches, worn in place of normal pouches, were designed to carry various explosive components as well as the pionier's gas mask and rifle ammunition.

The backpack fastened to the rings of the combat support straps. It was intended to carry further charges as well as the mess can and shelter quarter. His water bottle is clipped to his bread bag.

His weapon is the standard Karabiner 98K and an M1939 Smoke Stick Grenade is tucked into his belt. He carries a 'Teller Mine' 35.

SS-Panzergrenadier, 12th SS Panzer Division 'Hitlerjugend', Normandy 1944

By 1944 a wide variety of camouflage clothing was worn by Waffen-SS combat troops. This young machine gunner wears a typical combination of M1942 smock and M44 trousers.

The M1942 smock (here in 'blurred edge') was now common and was worn alongside previous variants. The 'dot' pattern trousers were part of the M44 Camouflage Drill Uniform which had a matching 4-pocket tunic. These could be worn over or in place of the field gray uniform. This camouflage outfit was designed with the intention of replacing all other camouflage gear. In reality the M44 uniform was just one more variation of Waffen-SS camouflage gear and was worn as illustrated.

Note that the helmet cover now has foliage loops attached and the marching boot was largely replaced with ankle-boots and canvas gaiters.

The standard equipment of a machine gunner is worn with his MG parts pouch on his right hip and a P38 holster on the left. Also attached to his belt are his bread bag with a water bottle and mess tin and a folding shovel.

It was common for HJ troops to darken their faces with charcoal or similar. His MG42 is fitted with a 50 round 'assault' drum.

SS-Schütze, Germany 1945

There is nothing specific that would identify this 'veteran' with a particular front. But for his Panzerfaust 60 (which was first issued in mid 1944) the time could be 1945.

The Waffen-SS had recognized the sound design of the Army's reversible winter uniform which first appeared in late 1942. By the next winter it was being produced in Waffen-SS camouflage material (primarily in brown 'oak leaf' and 'blurred edge' patterns). The only obvious design difference was the pointed pocket flaps on the Waffen-SS type. Note that the drawstring of the hood is missing and the white side of the waist tape is showing under the belt buckle.

The collar of his field gray uniform is barely visible beneath the wool toque worn around his neck. The M42 helmet likely has the SS decal on the right side. His felt and leather boots were common winter footwear after the winter of 42/43.

Standard rifleman's equipment is worn and with his Karabiner 98K slung, he carries a box of MG ammunition and the previously mentioned Panzerfaust 60.

This battery of 8cm sGrW 34 mortars was photographed after having dug in on a hillside where it could provide support for the infantry. As the photo indicates, the four-mortar battery has entrenched with only a small space between the mortars. Though commonly done, this tactic could result in heavy losses when the position came under enemy fire.

SS troops gather around a gramophone and records that arrived in a large parcel from home. We don't know whether the records are of Hitler's speeches, military marches or Wagner compositions, but it is a safe bet that one of the songs is the 'greatest hit' of World War Two, 'Lili Marlene', a song that was so popular it was played and sung by the soldiers of both the Axis and Allied forces. The soldiers here are wearing the special type of winter uniform that was introduced by the SS troops during WWII and is still worn by a few modern armies, including the U.S. Army.

This photo gives a good view of the fur-lined SS jackets, which have a distinct civilian appearance. The SS military clothing was the first comfortable and functional camouflaged combat uniforms widely worn by divisions in action. It is interesting to remember that this sort of uniform was unusual for the German Army, whose tradition-minded officers thought that soldiers ought to look proud and serious in their uniforms. They also believed that soldiers should fight and die in battle wearing nice-looking uniforms, not comfortable ones.

Two members of an MG42 team look up in relief to see the arrival of air support. Both soldiers are wearing reversible uniforms — gray for the autumn and white for the winter. During wet weather, however, both sides changed color very quickly, as can be seen by the way the coat on the soldier in the foreground has lost its original color. From the number of discarded empty ammunition boxes and the many spent cartridges on the ground beneath the gun barrel, it is clear that this team has been involved in some heated combat.

With the arrival of winter, an SS man whitewashes a PAK 40 gun. Note that even the wheels receive a coat of camouflage. Both of the soldiers in the foreground are wearing the autumn/winter reversible camouflage uniforms. The second soldier also wears the overjacket with gray fur in the hood.

An SS-Untersturmführer (2nd Lieutenant) gives orders to the StuG commanders in his battery. Note the unusual appearance of the soldier in the middle. By 1943, StuG IIIs had begun to be more prevalent in the SS divisions, where they were used as an assault gun, a Panzerjäger (tank hunter) . . . and even as a tank sometimes.

A salvo of rockets from a Nebelwerfer sails over the Russian winter landscape. This particular artillery piece, which had a rapid rate of fire (108 rounds in 10 seconds) posed a real danger to any enemy troops who happened to be positioned under the rain of these missiles.

Here a StuG crew prepares to go into action. The commander at left is putting on a reversible winter uniform, with the autumn side in, over the standard gray jacket worn by armored troops. The checkered texture on the armor of the assault gun is *Zimmerit*, a paste that was applied to protect the armored vehicle against antitank mines.

Gathered atop their StuG, members of the assault gun crew pay close attention to their commander as he reviews the plan of action for their upcoming mission. Note that the SS crew second from right wears the simple white smock meant only for camouflage purposes.

Another StuG crew prepares their vehicle for action. Note the atypical, almost chaotic camouflage pattern painted in brown on this assault gun. All first-rate SS divisions had sub-units of StuGs for tank destroying and infantry support duties since the time they were reorganized in 1940/1941.

SS-Hauptscharführer (Master-Sergeant) Gustaw Schreiber points to the spot where a Soviet bullet hit the Gewehr 43 semi-automatic rifle that belonged to one of his best soldiers from the 'Westland' Regiment of the 'Wiking' Division while the unit fought in southwestern Ukraine in March 1944. Schreiber was decorated with the Knight's Cross on 6 December 1943 for successfully defending the Kharkov-Poltava rail line during the Russian offensive in the autumn of 1943.

This pensive motorcycle soldier sits astride his BMW dressed in a sheepskin jacket covered by a winter camouflage jacket. Compared to the uniforms worn by the motorcyclists at the beginning of the war, this particular style is a noticeable departure. Note the mittens that keep his fingers nimble enough to operate the clutch.

An MG 42 squad, probably from II.SS-Panzer Korps, march into a new combat position east of the Lvov area early in the spring of 1944. All the soldiers carry ammunition boxes for the machine gun and wear the same uniform, i.e., camouflage smocks over standard field gray overcoats.

Vehicles of the 9th SS Panzer Division 'Hohenstaufen' and 10th SS Panzer Division 'Frundsberg' (part of the II.SS-Panzer Korps) struggle to cross a muddy field east of Lvov in April 1944 during the Russian spring offensive. The Tiger in the foreground carries the three-digit tactical number '214'. Note that the first digit is twice the size of the two others, which was the style of numbering the tanks in s.Pz.Abt.507.

Motorized SS troops from II.SS-Panzer Korps enter a city in western Ukraine in April 1944. The Sd.Kfz. 251 seen at the right is devoid of any camouflage — the typical result of a unit suffering from a lack of preparation time prior to combat. Despite the defeats the German Army was experiencing on the Russian Front at this time, these soldiers seem to be in good spirits.

SS-Obersturmführer (1st Lieutenant) Willi Hein poses beside the turret of his Pz.Kpfw. V 'Panther' just after receiving the Knight's Cross on 4 May 1944 while he was a staff officer in 2nd Company of a Panzer Regiment in 5th SS Panzer Division 'Wiking'. There were five other officers of Pz.Rgt.5 from this division decorated with the Knight's Cross for participation in the heavy fighting in the Kovel area during April-May 1944.

The only paratroop unit in the SS was the famous 500th *Fallschirmjäger-Bataillion*, part of which was a penal battalion, which took part in the raid on partisan leader Tito's headquarters in Drvar in the spring of 1944. In this photo, SS paratroops are seen undergoing training.

Here we see the 500th Fallschirmjäger Battalion in action. After the glider forces had landed, the paratroops were dropped from Ju52s. That moment is shown in this photo. Note the DFS230 glider in the foreground. Though the mission against Tito's headquarters was not completely successful (due to mistakes made by the leadership), the action was one of the best of World War Two.

The bitter fighting against partisans went on throughout the whole of 1943 and 1944 in Yugoslavia, as well. Here an MG30(t) team from the 7th SS Freiwilligen-Gebirgs Division 'Prinz Eugen' guards a mountain road. These soldiers, who were ethnic Germans living in the Balkans, wear camouflaged field caps and smocks over their overcoats. Just as on the Eastern Front, many victims of the partisan warfare in the Balkans were caused not by the SS but by the opposing native factions. However, many soldiers from the 'Prinz Eugen' Division were tried and executed for committing atrocities.

This photograph shows an officer of the reconnaissance unit of the 'Prinz Eugen' Division giving orders from his armored vehicle during an advance to the front lines. Note the *Edelweiss* flower insignia, the identification badge of the mountain troops, on the side of his field cap. The 'Prinz Eugen' Division was reinforced in 1943 and 1944 with two smaller divisions — the 13th and 21st, but 'Prinz Eugen' is the best remembered unit in the Balkans during World War Two.

A patrol of SS men uses a Schwimmwagen to traverse the ocean to reconnoiter a Greek ship anchored offshore. This photo is an interesting study of the contrast between traditional and modern amphibious vessels. As is often the case, warfare can be a catalyst for technological advances.

SS mountain troops welcome a supply of ammunition and weapons delivered by an Opel Blitz truck. Note the artillery piece under the tarp on the truck — it could be a 7.5cm leIG 18 light gun installed on the carriage of a 2.8cm PzB 41.

A high-ranking member of the NSKK (National Socialist Motor Corps) who has volunteered to serve in an SS unit secures a block against the tire of a truck being transported on a flatbed rail car. His field cap bears the insignia of a mountain trooper, but his sleeve insignia — the NSKK eagle arm badge and the NSKK Qualified Driver's insignia — confirm his Motor Corps background.

An SS soldier from a second-line unit reads a list of attractions featured at a nearby lily brook. The lack of field equipment, the holstered pistol and the style of uniform hint that this man may belong to a police unit.

The shortage in manpower that grew more severe as the war progressed compelled Himmler to recruit SS divisions from among the *Volksdeutsche*, the ethnic Germans located in occupied territory. During the Russian campaign, volunteers from non-Nordic locations such as the Ukraine were allowed to join. In early spring of 1944, Reichsführer-SS (Field Marshal) Heinrich Himmler (in overcoat) was photographed as he observed the training on a PAK 40 gun of soldiers of the 14th Waffen-Grenadier Division der SS 'Galitzien' (later changed to 'Ukranien'), which was composed of Ukranians located behind German lines.

The 14th Waffen-Grenadier Division der SS was one of three units organized with troops recruited from the Slavic nations who shared the German point of view toward the Russians. Here some of the Ukrainian soldiers train in the marshy swamps that protected the division's positions from partisan assaults.

Note that these Ukrainian SS men have been issued the same uniforms, armament, and equipment as the soldiers belonging to the other SS divisions. They even have received netting to protect their faces, which they have pushed back over their helmets. This additional piece of personal camouflage was quite commonly used in some sub-units, but it was often lost by the soldiers during hard campaigning.

The Croatians and Ukrainians had been the best German allies since before the war, with the Latvians being the most Germanic of the Slavic peoples. Here a squad of Ukrainian volunteers advance up a slope toward a well-concealed machine-gun nest during training exercises.

Aufklärungsabteilung (reconnaissance unit) troops from the 'Galitzien' Division perform river crossing exercises in a Schwimmwagen vehicle. The resourceful Ukrainians have covered the hood of the vehicle with a *zeltbahn* (shelter half) as a means of camouflage.

Concealed under tree branches and miscellaneous foliage, a Schwimmwagen operated by Ukrainian soldiers from the 14th Waffen-Grenadier Division der SS edges closer and closer to the opposite shore. Unfortunately, despite their training, the performance of the East European SS men rarely lived up to Himmler's expectations.

Looking almost as capable as veteran troops of the Waffen-SS, a platoon of Ukrainian volunteers perform a simulation of an amphibious assault of enemy river bank. Note how high the water reaches on each side of the vehicles.

This action scene shows reconnaissance troops of the 'Galitzien' Division in the midst of a training exercise as they practice how to capture an undamaged bridge. The scene would be an unusual subject for those readers interested in historical scale modeling.

A Ukrainian SS man demonstrates the simplest method of transporting a motorcycle across a river. Note how the propeller is lifted away from the mud until the Schwimmwagen reaches deeper water where it can be lowered again.

An SS NCO and his 'best friend' relax at the bank of a river after a long, hot training exercise. From the appearance of the dog's fur, it appears that both of them have made use of the water to cool off and wash up. Note the pouch the SS man wears on his hip.

Following the end of the training exercises, Reichsführer-SS Himmler, who offers the Nazi salute while standing in his touring car at left, takes some time to review the reconnaissance battalion of the 'Galitzien' Division. Near the car, wearing a light overcoat, is the Galician governor, SS-Brigadeführer (Brigadier) Wächter.

The parade of the Ukrainian troops of the recce battalion of the 'Galitzien' Division continues as the beauties of the division— the cavalry squadron— pass in review in front of Heinrich Himmler. Note the 'pea' pattern camouflage on the tunics worn by the horsemen.

If the 'Galitzien' Division was the first Slavic front-line formation in the SS, one of the last ones was the 30th Waffen-Grenadier Division der SS, which was incorporated with great difficulty. It was composed of Belorussians who had served in rear echelon security units. There were plans to reorganize all Russian units under the command of General Vlassov (who we can see in this photo), but the plan was never finalized. From the beginning, the main obstacle to the plan was Adolf Hitler, who did not want any Eastern allies, particularly Russian, then Himmler felt the same way for many months.

Another non-German unit, the 33rd Waffen-Grenadier Division der SS 'Charlemagne', was probably even more disliked by Hitler than the Slavic units. Perhaps he would have been very surprised and happy to know that the French SS men were the bravest and most stalwart defenders of Berlin at the end of the war. Visible on the arm of the soldier at right is the arm shield identifying him as a volunteer from France. Worth remembering is that not many soldiers from the larger SS units wore such national insignia.

Seen here on the left sleeve of the soldier on the right (below the national eagle) is another such foreign volunteer arm shield, this one featuring the Latvian colors of 15th Waffen-Grenadier Division der SS. After the bitter defeat suffered in the summer of 1944, units formed from volunteers in the Baltic nations lost many soldiers due to desertion, but those who remained fought bravely to the end.

Led by a Pz.Kpfw. III, an SS machine-gun squad uses a cornfield for a short cut to the front lines somewhere in the western part of the Soviet Union in the summer of 1944. Note how the tall corn stalks obscure the troops from view.

Using a demolished T-34 for cover, a trio of SS soldiers from the 'Totenkopf' Division consult a map, which has been heavily censored by the press staff. Note that the soldier in the middle has a 'Nazi flag' SS decal on his helmet, which was a vary rare marking even before 1944.

A machine-gun team armed with an MG42 with a drum magazine dig in somewhere on the Estonian-Russian border in the summer of 1944. Note that the soldier at the extreme right is wearing a mosquito net for protection against the gnats, which were very troublesome to the troops at this time of the year. The nets were manufactured in different shades of green and brown in a variety of sizes that allowed the soldiers to actually cover their whole head, even while wearing a helmet, as is seen in this photograph.

Crouched in the tall grass of a river bank behind a machine-gun squad, we get a soldier's-eye view of troop movement during the fighting in the Eastern Front in the summer of 1944. The way these SS men keep their heads down lets us know that danger is not far distant.

The new antitank weapon in 1944 was the 8.8cm RpzB 54 *Panzerschreck*. Big and heavy, and operated by a two-man crew, it was not as simple a weapon as the smaller *Panzerfaust* single-shot rocket launcher, but it was a valuable weapon to the troops because of the damage it could inflict on the enemy. In the final months of the war, the Panzerschreck (or the Panzerfaust) was the only type of antitank weapon carried by some minor SS units. As can be seen in the photo, such antitank teams carried only pistols for self-defense.

The crew of Tiger number '901' is seen here during a moment of relaxation in the summer of 1944. The SS man in the foreground is the driver. Behind him, wearing the ubiquitous officer's and NCO's field cap, is the commander of the tank.

This photo shows a Panzerschreck being operated in a prone position. Note the equipment on the soldier's back — on top of it is a loaf of bread. The Panzerschreck seen here is an old one, and it has lost some of its sandy paint job. Contemporary photos exist that show these bazookas painted with one or two additional camouflage colors.

A column of SS troops advances toward enemy lines, glancing at the camera as they pass. Interestingly, the officer in the lead wears a field cap made from a much lighter colored material than the rest of his men. Note the variety of weapons they carry — Mauser rifles, MP40s, MG42s, and even a Panzerfaust.

SS-Obergruppenführer (Lieutenant-General) Josef 'Sepp' Dietrich (right) and Minster of Armaments and War Production Albert Speer (center) are seen here not long before the beginning of operations on the Western Front in Normandy. Speer later claimed that Dietrich complained that the SS troops under his command had not been as tough in combat against the U.S. Army as they had been while battling the Russians.

Several high-ranking officers of the German forces in France watch military exercises from a half-track tractor before the Allied landing in Normandy. At the extreme left is the famous General-Feldmarschall Gerd von Rundstedt. Next to him are: (left to right) SS-Sturmbannführer (Major) Hubert Meyer, SS-Oberstgruppenführer (General) Josef Dietrich and SS-Oberführer (Senior General) Fritz Witt, the commander of 'Hitlerjugend' Division.

SS-Brigadeführer (Brigadier-General) Werner Ostendorff, commander of the 17th SS Panzergrenadier Division 'Götz von Berlichingen', is seen here talking to Major von der Heydte from the II.Fallshirmjäger Korps in the Carentan area in June 1944. A few days after this photo was taken, Ostendorff was badly wounded during the heavy fighting in the St. Lo region of France. He was decorated with the Knight's Cross on 13 September 1941 for action in the Jelnia area of Russia.

In early July 1944, an Sd.Kfz. 251 belonging to an SS reconnaissance unit is used to transport British prisoners to a command point for interrogation. The armored half-track is camouflaged with green and brown paint over a background of sand.

This photograph was taken somewhere on the Western Front very early in July 1994. It features, from left to right, the commander of the I.SS-Panzer Korps, SS-Oberstgruppenführer (General) Josef 'Sepp' Dietrich, the commander of OB West, General-Feldmarschall Gunther von Kluge and the commander of Pz.Kp. West, Heinrich Eberwach.

Heavy fighting took place in the area around Caen, France in July 1944. During the fighting in the Normandy campaign, soldiers of *Das Heer* (German Army) and the SS armored troops proved themselves to be (arguably) better warriors than the allied soldiers they faced. Overwhelmed by superior numbers, they fought hard and well, causing a great deal of grief and inflicting many casualties on the Allies in the west.

This unusual photo shows the staff car of 'Sepp' Dietrich moments after it was attacked by allied fighters and set ablaze. The fire was put out with the help of French villagers. SS-Oberstgruppenführer Dietrich (at left with hands on his hips) was able to flee the vehicle and save his life. Note the irritated look on his face.

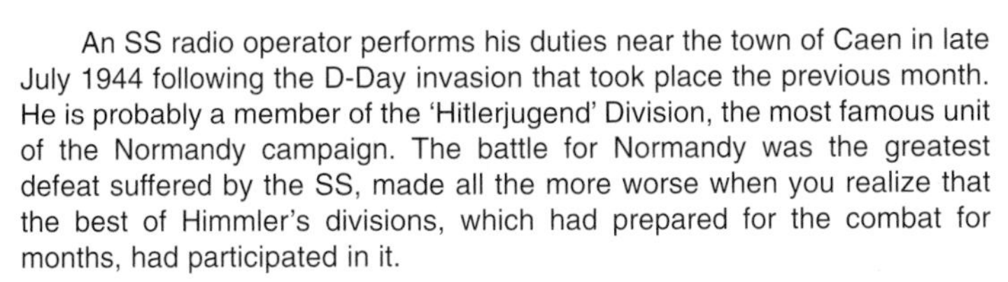

An SS radio operator performs his duties near the town of Caen in late July 1944 following the D-Day invasion that took place the previous month. He is probably a member of the 'Hitlerjugend' Division, the most famous unit of the Normandy campaign. The battle for Normandy was the greatest defeat suffered by the SS, made all the more worse when you realize that the best of Himmler's divisions, which had prepared for the combat for months, had participated in it.

Here is a good example of the way SS troops looked in the field (except for the non-issue bunch of flowers stuck in the old-style camouflage smock worn by the soldier at left). The soldier at right, who carries a small Panzerfaust 30 antitank weapon, has arranged his equipment in a rather unusual fashion. Both men have their regulation mosquito nets pushed back over

The commander of the 1st SS Panzer Division 'Leibstandarte Adolf Hitler' (LAH) just after receiving the *Brillanten* to the Knight's Cross on 6 August 1944 for the two months of fighting in the Caen area. There is no doubt that this defensive operation of the SS was a great military performance, even though all of Dietrich's 6.Pz.Armee were annihilated. One must remember that it was General Bernard L. Montgomery who gave a great deal of support to the opponents of the SS.

Waffen-SS troops crouch in the grass as they prepare to go into combat, with some welcome support from a pair of StuG IV assault guns. Note that a couple of soldiers have painted their helmets in a two-tone camouflage scheme.

Soldiers of the 28th SS Freiwilligen-Panzergrenadier Division 'Wallonien' (this division never exceeded regimental strength), who fought hard in the Riga area, inspect a battlefield and cautiously approach an IS-2 to find out if anyone is 'at home'. The first battle for Riga was won by the Germans, who caused the advancing Soviet tank formations to suffer heavy losses.

During the fighting for the city of Riga, the members of an SS Panzerschreck team stealthily advance through the cover of trees and grass to ply their deadly trade against an unwary Soviet tank. Note the large ammunition box that houses the rockets for the antitank weapon.

Wearing the standard SS camouflage smock, a member of the 28th SS Freiwilligen-Panzergrenadier Division 'Wallonien', probably a Belgian, stands atop a blown-up Russian T-34-85 tank to inspect the work of an antitank team.

These two photos show the effectiveness of the Panzerschreck antitank weapon. In each one, SS men from the 28th SS Freiwilligen-Panzergrenadier Division 'Wallonien' cautiously approach the wreckage of Russian IS-2 heavy tanks that have been set ablaze and are belching smoke after being neutralized by an SS Panzerschreck team.

Ernst Schachinger, a 21-year-old from Vienna, Austria, found yet another new way to battle the enemies of the Third Reich. After having served in Waffen-SS units for four years, he volunteered to be the first SS man to participate in a special *Kriegsmarine* (German Navy) unit of one-man U-boats. Here Schachinger (far right) talks with a couple of his comrades.

In his service in the SS, Ernst Schachinger had fought on all fronts. This photo shows the tiny *Einmanntorpedo* (one-man torpedo) mini-U-boat in which the young Ernst Schachinger set out to sea. After sinking a 'liberty' ship, the 'SS sailor' was decorated with the German Cross in Gold.

While thousands of people from the Eastern nations were willing to sacrifice their lives for Hitler, thousands more fought against him in partisan units. Here one of the Eastern SS men cautiously wades through knee-high water in search of fellow countrymen who fail to share his politics.

Following some bitter fighting against the Soviets, members of two *Aufklärungsabteilungen* from the 'Wiking' and 'Totenkopf' Divisions meet somewhere in Poland in August 1944. In the foreground are two armored cars that were standard equipment of the recce troops — an Sd.Kfz. 223 and an Sd.Kfz. 222.

SS men and police units formed from volunteers in the occupied countries played an active part in anti-partisan operations. Here a squad of volunteer SS men chase after some fleeing partisans. The variety in their uniforms and equipment indicates that the soldiers belong to a second-class unit.

One of the largest anti-partisan operations of World War Two was the battle for Warsaw in August-September 1944. Does this photo show young SS soldiers enjoying a success? Not at all. They are Polish partisans from the underground army who fought for Warsaw in SS uniforms captured from POWs and supply trains abandoned in the city. The soldier at the right even has the field-gray uniform of the 'Totenkopf' Division, complete with collar patches. It isn't hard to guess what the German soldiers thought about this practice and why such partisans were shot on the spot with no questions asked.

Here a group of SS men who fell into the hands of the Polish during the fighting in Warsaw dejectedly share a meal. At the beginning of the uprising, German POWs were treated well, partly for propaganda purposes. Later, though, when the underground army began to suffer due to the lack of water, food and medical supplies, the fate of the POWs grew worse. During the two months of battle, the German Army recorded about 7,000 soldiers missing. Their fate is not known, but it is possible that Polish soldiers killed a number of them after capture.

Reichsjugendführer Artur Axmann (left) decorates a young soldier from the 12th SS Panzer Division 'Hitlerjugend' with the *Eisernkreuz* (Iron Cross) during an inspection of the division on 19 September 1944, when what was left of the division was regrouped following the collapse at Normandy. The personnel of the 'Hitlerjugend' Division consisted for the most part of former Hitler Youth members.

SS-Obersturmbannführer (Lieutenant-Colonel) Herald Riipalu explains to other SS officers the proper procedure for using a Panzerfaust rocket launcher. Riipalu was decorated with the Knight's Cross on 11 September 1944 for successfully leading the SS Waffen-Grenadier Regiment 45 of the Estonian 20th Waffen-Grenadier Division der SS during the fighting in the Riga area. This photo was taken in November 1944.

Seen here are the smoldering remains of a Soviet aircraft shot down by SS soldiers in late autumn 1944. The wreckage is of a Bell P-39 'Airacobra' that was used by the Soviet Air Force. The manner in which the soldier at right carries his hand grenades, much like the bandoleer of a 17th century warrior, is noteworthy.

SS-Gruppenführer (Major General) Heinz Reinefarth won oak leaves for his Knight's Cross on 4 October 1944 for his participation in the brutal fighting in Warsaw, where he commanded a special battle group composed of SS and Wehrmacht troops. During the two months of combat, German troops slaughtered up to 170,000-180,000 POWs and civilians; another 20,000-30,000 were killed in combat. Here we see Reinefarth training new SS soldiers in December 1944.

The final large-scale operation in which the SS took part prior to the end of the war was in Hungary in January 1945. A few sub-units of these units were used to support Eichmann's extermination operations against the Jews. Here a PAK 40 gun from one of the SS divisions is put to use in the battle for Budapest in early 1945.

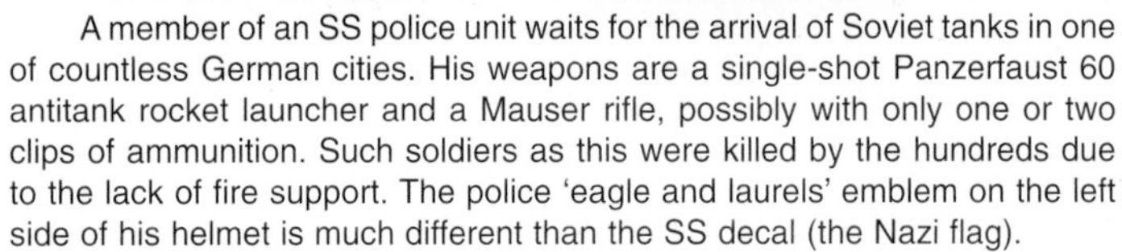

A member of an SS police unit waits for the arrival of Soviet tanks in one of countless German cities. His weapons are a single-shot Panzerfaust 60 antitank rocket launcher and a Mauser rifle, possibly with only one or two clips of ammunition. Such soldiers as this were killed by the hundreds due to the lack of fire support. The police 'eagle and laurels' emblem on the left side of his helmet is much different than the SS decal (the Nazi flag).

This atypical warrior is an older gentleman belonging to a field police unit. Dressed in a new, clean uniform (including polished buttons and boots), he appears to be a most determined tank hunter. He is armed with a Panzerfaust 60 and a pistol, with additional pistol ammo in a cartridge pouch on his belt. His helmet features the Nazi flag emblem of the SS, but on the opposite side of where it is usually located.

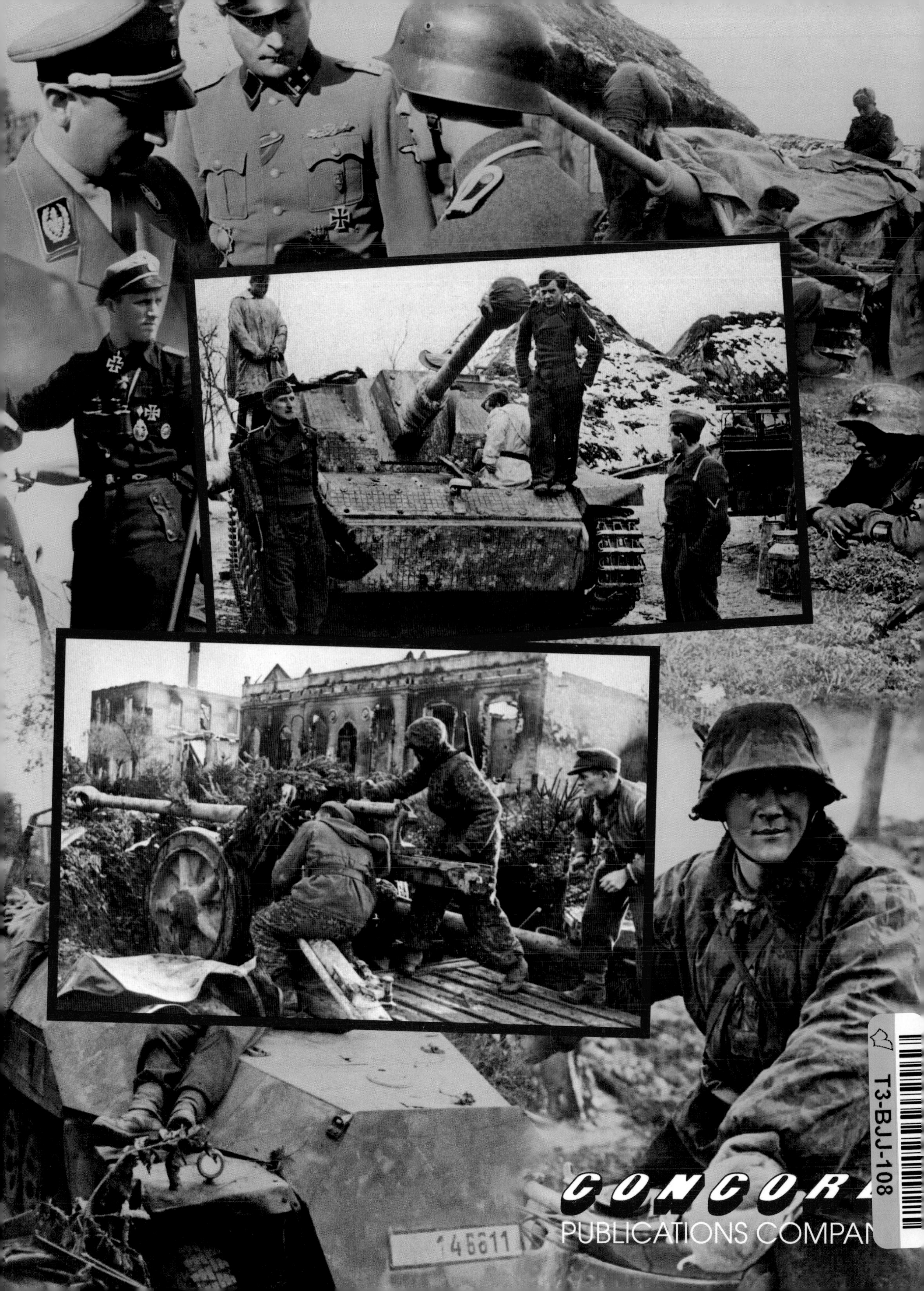
CONCOR
PUBLICATIONS COMPAN
146611
T3-BJJ-108